"Because of Jesus Christ I am"......

Great benefits and privileges
Of being in Christ

40 Days Study Devotions
By Mary Favors

All copyrights© 2013 Mary Favors ISBN: *978-0-9848389-3-6*

Bible used: 21st Century King James Version (KJ21), American Standard Version (ASV), Amplified Bible (AMP), Common English Bible (CEB), Complete Jewish Bible (CJB), Holman Christian Standard Bible(HCSB), King James Version (KJV), The Message (MSG), New American Standard Bible (NASB), New King James Version (NKJV), New Living Translation (NLT)

I am born again and a believer in all Jesus Christ did for me by the way of the cross. Are you born again in Jesus Christ?" If not, "Would like to become a member of the body of Christ?"

You may ask, "What does it mean to be born again?"

The term "born again" first appears in the Bible in John chapter three......
There was a man named Nicodemus, a Jewish religious leader who was a Pharisee. After dark one evening, he came to speak with Jesus. "Rabbi," he said, "we all know that God has sent you to teach us. Your miraculous signs are evidence that God is with you. "Jesus replied, "I tell you the truth, unless you are born again, you cannot see the Kingdom of God." "What do you mean?" exclaimed Nicodemus. "How can an old man go back into his mother's womb and be born again?" Jesus replied, "I assure you, no one can enter the Kingdom of God without being born of water and the Spirit. Humans can reproduce only human life, but the Holy Spirit gives birth to spiritual life So don't be surprised when I say, 'You must be born again.'
To be "born again" is when Jesus Christ comes into your body to live, literally in the form of the Spirit of God. Romans 8:9 say, "But you are not controlled by your sinful nature. You are controlled by the Spirit if you have the Spirit of God living in you. (And remember that those who do not have the Spirit of Christ living in them do not belong to him at all). To understand what it means to be born again, it is necessary to understand that there are two births. The "first" birth is the physical birth when you were born into the world from your mother and father. When the Bible speaks of being "born of water" it is speaking about the physical birth (not baptism). The "second" birth is a spiritual birth, which means to be born of the "Spirit" (that is, God's Holy Spirit).

Why does a person need to be born spiritually? God will never force anyone to accept Jesus as their Savior, He invites anyone who wants to be forgiven of their sins and to receive Salvation and not perish but have eternal life. John 3:16-21 (NLT) [16] "For God loved the world so much that he gave His one and only Son, so that everyone who believes in Him will not perish but have eternal life. [17] God sent his Son into the world not to judge the world, but to save the world through him. [18] "There is no judgment against anyone who believes in Him. But anyone who does not believe in Him has already been judged for not believing in God's one and only Son. [19] And the judgment is based on this fact: God's Light came into the world, but people loved the darkness more than the Light, for their actions were evil. [20] All who do evil hate the Light and refuse to go near it for fear their sins will be exposed. [21] But those who do what is right come to the Light so others can see that they are doing what God wants." Salvation is a gift paid by the precious blood of Jesus Christ. We must accept God's gift of eternal life before we die then the gift will be forever forfeited. So you can surrender to life or death. "The choose is your."

How did every person become sinners? Because of disobedience:

God commanded Adam and Eve not to eat of the fruit from the tree. But
the LORD God warned him, "You may freely eat the fruit of every tree in the garden— [17] except the tree of the knowledge of good and evil. If you eat its fruit, you are sure to die." (Genesis 2: 16 – 17)

Adam and Eve did not physically die the day they ate from the tree. But a spiritual death took place, because of disobeying God's command. Because Adam sinned; sin and death entered the human race. The Bible teaches that from Adam until present time, mankind has been born spiritually dead meaning separated, alienated, estranged from God. This is why humanity must be born again. By having faith in Jesus Christ as our Savior and there by receiving the Holy Spirit of God which make us alive again (quickened the Bible says). We are saved and born again by repenting of our sins and unbelief and believing the Gospel the Good News that Jesus died, was buried and raised from the dead on third day. This means that anyone who belongs to Christ has become a new person. The old life is gone; a new life has begun! 2 Corinthians 5:17 (NLT)

Salvation Prayer
Dear God,
I come to You in the Name of Jesus. I admit that I am not right with You and I want to be right with You. I ask You to forgive me of all my sins. I denounce Satan and all his works. The Bible says if I confess with my mouth that "Jesus is Lord," and I believe in my heart that God raised Him from the dead, I will be saved. (Rom. 10:9) I believe with my heart and I confess with my mouth that Jesus is the Lord and Savior of my life. Thank You for saving me!
In Jesus' Name I pray. Amen.

Receive God Holy Spirit. As His child, your loving heavenly Father wants to give you the supernatural power you need to live this new life.
For every one that asketh receiveth; and he that seeketh findeth; and to him that knocketh it shall be opened... If ye...know how to give good gifts unto your children: how much more shall your heavenly Father give the Holy Spirit to them that ask him? (LUKE 11:10 - 13)

All you have to do is ask, believe, and receive! Pray, Father, I recognize my need for Your power to live this new life. Please fill me with Your Holy Spirit. By faith, I receive Him right now! Thank You for baptizing me. Holy Spirit, You are welcome in my life.

Congratulations! Now you're filled with God's supernatural power. Some syllables from a language you don't recognize will rise up from your heart to your mouth. (Read 1 Cor. 14:14) As you speak them out loud by faith, you're releasing God's power from within and building yourself up in the Spirit. (Read v. 4) You can do this whenever and wherever you like.

It doesn't really matter whether you felt anything or not when you prayed to receive the Lord and His Spirit. If you believed in your heart that you received, then God's Word promises you did. "Therefore I say unto you, what things so ever you desire, when ye pray, believe that ye receive them, and ye shall have them" (Read Mark 11:24) God always honors His Word; believe it! Pray and ask the Father to give you a church home. Read the Book of John; I John, II John; and III John.

Now you can truly say
"Because of Jesus Christ I am"......

Day 1   *I am the righteousness of God!*

    This is an important summary of the gospel message. The verse explains how God imputed (to attribute a usually undesirable action or event to somebody) our sin to Christ. God as judge assigned the responsibility of our sin to Christ making it possible for Him to be punished justly for that sin. The verse shows that Christ was our substitute, accepting the penalty of sin in our place.

    We might become the righteousness of God. Not only did God impute our sin to Christ, He also imputed Christ's perfect righteousness to us (that is, He counted His righteousness belonging to us). This imputation is the basis for the progressive realization of God's righteousness in our moral character. Our thoughts and deeds are sanctified in increasing measure until we receive perfect righteousness in heaven.

Read and write II Corinthians 5:21; Romans 3: 20 - 23

_____
_____
_____
_____
_____
_____
_____
_____
_____
_____
_____
_____
_____
_____
_____
_____
_____
_____
_____
_____

The full right reserved for one who has grown up is adoption as a son and receiving the inheritance.

There is only one condition for the experience of the Spirit in our hearts: *Because you are sons, God sent the Spirit of His Son into our hearts.* There is no other prerequisite for this experience of the Spirit besides receiving the gift of adoption. We do not need to go through a series of steps, recite special prayers or meet extra conditions. God sends the Spirit of His Son into our heart for one reason: because He adopted us into His family.

To view adoption and reception of the Spirit as two separate stages in the Christian life tears apart the jointed relation of adoption and the sending of the Spirit. Paul's unique title for the Spirit here, *Spirit of His Son,* emphasizes the unity of the experience of adoption and the experience of the Spirit.

Read and write Galatians 4: 4 -7

_____

_____

_____

_____

_____

_____

_____

_____

_____

_____

_____

_____

_____

_____

_____

_____

_____

_____

_____

_____

_____

_____

Day 3 — I am a joint-heir with Jesus!

What does it mean to be joint- heir with Jesus and the benefits?
To be in Christ is to be an heir. Now we are sons of God through faith in Christ Jesus. When we were baptized into Christ we have put on Christ. We have the authority God gave Jesus while He was in this world. "The Spirit Himself bears witness with our spirit that we are children of God, and if children, then heirs— heirs of God and joint heirs with Christ, if indeed we suffer with Him, that we may also be glorified together."
That's incredible! "Heirs of God and co-heirs with Christ" What does God plan to give us as our inheritance? Just as Jesus' inheritance of a resurrection from the dead and an everlasting kingdom was prophesied and known also to Christ.

I am an heir of Abraham's promise!

When we discuss the promises made unto the fathers (especially those that are related to Abraham), we often consider the 3rd chapter of Galatians. It is here we learn that the promises were to be fulfilled **through one special seed, which was Christ**. We are also told that those who are baptized into Christ will become "heirs according to the promise".

Then are ye Abraham's seed - The promise made to Abraham related to the Messiah. It was a promise that in Him all should be blessed. Abraham believed in that Messiah, and was well-known for his faith in him who was to come. If they believed in Christ, therefore, they showed that they were the spiritual descendants of Abraham. No matter whether they were Jews or Gentiles; whether they had been circumcised or not. Because of the promises God made to Abraham; because we believe in Jesus this make us heir of Abraham.

Read Galatians 3: 27 -29; Romans 8:16-17

_____
_____
_____
_____
_____
_____
_____
_____
_____
_____
_____
_____
_____
_____
_____
_____

The gospel does not pronounce condemnation like the Law. Its function is to pardon; the function of the law is to condemn. Condemnation is being declared guilty because you have broken the law of God and are deserving of the penalty of spiritual death. It is the breaking of God's law that makes you feel guilty. Then, because of that guilt, and because God is just, it means that you are deserving of death for breaking the law. The resulting feeling is condemnation. The Law never deliverance, but always condemns; the object of grace is to free from condemnation, and to set the soul at liberty because of the intervention of Jesus Christ. You are not condemned for your past, you are not condemned for your current struggles, and you are not going to be condemned in the future. Jesus Christ came through the love of God so that men and women could be free from condemnation. That is the good news of the Gospel.

Read and write Romans 8:1 Romans 7:23-25

_____
_____
_____
_____
_____
_____
_____
_____
_____
_____
_____
_____
_____
_____
_____
_____
_____
_____
_____
_____

When you hear the word "rooted" you usually think of a tree. When you plant a tree, it is easy to pull it out of the ground after the first few days. But it will be nearly impossible to pull the tree out once it is properly rooted.

Apostle Paul advises being firmly rooted in the Lord: "[Be] rooted and built up in Him and established in the faith." If this can be said of us, then nothing can cause us to be uprooted. It is therefore important that we are firmly rooted in our faith anyone who tries to pull us out then will be unsuccessful. Then no spirit can stand a chance against us because we are firmly rooted in the doctrine of Jesus Christ. But this is not always easy because Satan is constantly at work, and he seeks to pull us out of this firm grounding.

Oh, the joys of those who do not follow the advice of the wicked, or stand around with sinners, or join in with mockers. But they delight in the law of the LORD, meditating on it day and night. They are like trees planted along the riverbank, bearing fruit each season. Their leaves never wither, and they prosper in all they do.

Just as the trees need water to grow and can not live with out it. As believer we need Jesus He is our living water and we must abide and remain in Him day and night. Then and only then will you be rooted and built up and able to walk in faith so you may be established in Jesus. And it is impossible to please God without faith. Anyone who wants to come to Him must believe that God exists and that He rewards those who sincerely seek Him.

Read and write Ephesians 3:17; Matthew 15:13; Colossians 2:7

_____

_____

_____

_____

_____

_____

_____

_____

_____

_____

_____

_____

_____

It appears that all is of grace, because all our spiritual advantages are from God. We are His workmanship; He means in respect of the new creation; not only as men, but as saints. The new man is a new creature; and God is its Creator. It is a new birth, and we are born or begotten of His will. In Christ Jesus, that is, on the account of what He has done and suffered, and by the influence and operation of His blessed Spirit. "Unto good works" The apostle having before ascribed this change to divine grace in exclusion of works, lest he should seem thereby to discourage good works, he here observes that though the change is to be ascribed to nothing of that nature (for we are the workmanship of God), yet God, in His new creation, has designed and prepared us for good works: Created unto good works, with a design that we should be fruitful in them.

Wherever God by His grace implants good principles, they are intended to be for good works. *Which God hath before ordained*, that is, decreed and appointed. Or, the words may be read, "*To which God hath before prepared us,*" that is, by blessing us with the knowledge of His will and with the assistance of His Holy Spirit; and by producing such a change in us. "*That we should walk in them* or glorify God by an excellent conversation and by our perseverance in holiness."

Write the Definition for Workmanship: Read and write Ephesians 2:10

_____
_____
_____
_____
_____
_____
_____
_____
_____
_____
_____
_____
_____
_____
_____
_____
_____

Blessed is the one who does not walk in step with the wicked or stand in the way that sinners take or sit in the company of mockers, but whose delight is in the law of the LORD, and who meditates on His law day and night. That person is like a tree planted by streams of water, which yields its fruit in season and whose leaf does not wither—whatever they do prosper. Not so the wicked! They are like chaff that the wind blows away. Therefore the wicked will not stand in the judgment, or sinners in the assembly of the righteous. For the LORD watches over the way of the righteous but the way of the wicked leads to destruction. (Psalm 1)

But, when it comes to this matter of blessings, we often view them in the wrong light. Most often, we think of blessings as being those things that are physical and material in nature. For instance, if everyone in our household is well, we consider ourselves blessed. If there is money in the bank and the bills are paid, we say we are blessed. If we are living in a nice home and driving a good car, we equate that with blessing. And, I would have to agree that those things are blessings from the Lord. When reading Psalm chapter 1 we see the blessing are different.

Webster defines **"Blessed"** as, *"Of or enjoying happiness. Specifically enjoying the bliss of Heaven."* It carries the idea of that which *"brings pleasure, contentment, or good fortune."* Simply stated, it is that state of being that we all want to enjoy.

The Hebrew verb *barak* means to bless as seen in Genesis 12:2 but can also mean kneel as seen in Genesis 24:11. A related Hebrew word is *berakah* meaning a blessing or a gift or present. From this we can see the concrete meaning behind barak in the sense of a blessing. It is to bring a gift to another while kneeling out of respect. The extended meaning of this word is to do or give something of value to another. God "blesses" us by providing for our needs and we in turn "bless" God by giving Him ourselves as His servants.

Read and write Genesis 12:2; Genesis 24:11.

_____

_____

_____

_____

_____

Before the fall: **Pure & holy**	*After the fall:* **Corrupted & defaced**	*Through the cross:* **Renewed in Christ**
Holy, innocent: "God created man in His own image.... God saw everything that He had made, and indeed it was very good." **Gen 1:27, 31**	Driven by guilt and fear, quick to blame: "The woman *whom You* gave to be with me, *she gave* me of the tree, and I ate." **Gen 3:12**	The exchanged life: Christ's purity replaces our marred image: "I am crucified with Christ: nevertheless I live; yet not I, but **Christ liveth in me.**" **Gal 2:20**
Enjoyed the amazing blessing of God's holy presence and provisions	"...without Christ... and strangers from the covenants of promise, having no hope and without God in the world." **Eph 2:12**	"But now in Christ Jesus you who once were far off have been **brought near by the blood of Christ.**" **Eph 2:13** "There is therefore no condemnation to those who are in Christ Jesus, who do not walk according to the flesh, but according to the Spirit." **Rom 8:1**
"...they were both naked... and were **not ashamed.**" **Gen 2:25**	Adam felt shame: " I was afraid, because I was naked; and **I hid myself.**" **Gen 3:10**	No shame: "...you are in Christ Jesus, **who became for us... righteousness** and sanctification and redemption — that... "He who glories, let him glory in the Lord." **1 Cor. 1:30-31**
Had received perfect, uncorrupted life from God -- spiritual as well as physical	Spiritually dead: "**you... were dead in trespasses and sins,** in which you once walked according to the course of this world, according to... the spirit who now works in the sons of disobedience ...." **Eph 2:1-2**	New life in Christ: "But God, who is rich in mercy, because of His great love with which He loved us, even when we were dead in trespasses, made us **alive together with Christ.**" **Eph 2:4-6**
God's special creation, called to be God's friends and stewards of the rest of creation.	Under a curse: "...we all once conducted ourselves in the lusts of our flesh, fulfilling the desires of the flesh and of the mind, and were by nature **children of wrath.**"**Eph 2:3**	Freed from the curse: "For by grace you have been saved through faith, and that not of yourselves; it is the gift of God." **Eph 2:8**

Before the fall: Pure and holy	After the fall Corrupted & defaced	Through the cross: Renewed in Christ
No separation. Walked and talked with God, and wanted to do His will.	Separation from God: Unbelievers "walk in the futility of their mind, having their understanding darkened, being **alienated from the life of God....**" Eph 4:17-18	Separation unto God: "do not be conformed to this world, but be transformed by the renewing of your mind, that you may prove what is that good and acceptable and perfect will of God." **Rom 12:2** "...put on the new man who is renewed in knowledge according to the **image of Him** who created him." **Col 3:10**
Had original knowledge.	No understanding: "Professing to be wise, they became fools.... as they did not like to retain God in their knowledge, God gave them over to a **debased mind....**"Rom 1:22, 28	Spirit-given knowledge: "'Eye has not seen, nor ear heard... the things which God has prepared for those who love Him.' But God has revealed them to us through His Spirit." **1 Co 2:9-10** "...renewed in knowledge according to the **image of Him....**" **Col 3:10**
Motivated by love for God. Sought to please Him.	Driven by lusts: "Therefore God also gave them up to uncleanness, in the lusts of their hearts, to dishonor their bodies among themselves." **Ro 1:24**	Freed from lust: "...as Christ was raised from the dead by the glory of the Father, even so we also should walk in newness of life.... reckon yourselves to be dead indeed to sin, but alive to God in Christ Jesus our Lord." **Rom 6:4, 11**

Before the fall: Pure and holy	After the fall Corrupted & defaced	Through the cross: Renewed in Christ
Fully satisfied, all needs met.	Never satisfied: "...have given themselves over to lewdness, to work all uncleanness with **greediness.**" **Eph 4:19**	Fully satisfied: "my God shall supply all your need according to His riches in glory by Christ Jesus." **Phil 4:19**
Jesus -- eternal, pure, holy and righteous - manifests that image:" **He is the image of the invisible God....**" **Col 1:15**	"Our gospel is... veiled to those who are perishing, whose minds the god of this age has blinded, who do not believe, lest the light of the gospel of the glory of **Christ, who is the image of God,** should shine on them." **2 Co 4:3-4**	Our new image must be like Jesus: "For whom He foreknew, He also predestined to be **conformed to the image** of His Son." **Rom 8:29**

The only way a person is accepted in the beloved is "Christ alone;" is made our righteousness and results in our right relationship with God. Christ is of God "made unto us righteousness." If a right standing depended upon our faith or our faithfulness we would be eternally condemned. It depends upon Christ's................ righteousness accepted as His gift by faith. It does not depend upon our deeds, but upon the finished work of Christ. "You are complete in Christ." God sees nothing from His throne but Christ Jesus alone and Him crucified. And since the believer is in Him and one with Him, he shares Christ's place in the Father's heart. No matter how unworthy the believer is in himself, he may know without a doubt that he is "accepted in the Beloved."

poem called "In the Beloved"

"In the Beloved" accepted am I, risen ascended, and seated on high. Saved from all sin through His infinite grace; with the redeemed ones accorded a place. "In the Beloved" - How safe my retreat! "In the Beloved" - Accounted complete! Who can condemn me? In Him I am free! Savior and Keeper forever is He! "In the Beloved" I went to the tree, there in His person, by faith I now see Infinite wrath rolling over His head, Infinite grace, for He died in my stead! "In the Beloved" - God's.......... marvelous grace Calls me to dwell in this wonderful place! God sees my Savior, and then He sees me, "In the Beloved" accepted and free!

Read and write Ephesians 1: 4 - 7

_____

_____

_____

_____

_____

_____

_____

_____

_____

_____

_____

_____

_____

_____

No remission without redemption. It was by reason of sin that we were captivated, and we cannot be released from our captivity but by the remission of our sins. This redemption we have in Christ, and this remission through His blood. The guilt and the stain of sin can not be removed; only by the blood of Jesus. All our spiritual blessings flow down to us in that stream. This great benefit, which comes freely to us, was dearly bought and paid for by our blessed Lord; and yet it is according to the riches of God's grace.

Christ's satisfaction and God's rich grace are very consistent in the great affair of man's redemption. God was satisfied by Christ as our substitute and surety; but it was God's grace that would accept of a surety (payment), when He might have executed the severity and harshness of the law upon the transgressor, and it was rich grace to provide such a surety as His own Son, and freely to deliver Him up, when nothing of that nature could have entered into our thoughts, nor have been any otherwise found out for us. In this instance He has not only manifested riches of grace, but *has abounded towards us in all wisdom and prudence* and care.

Read and write Ephesians 1: 7, 8; Colossians 1:14

We were dead because of our sins, but God loved us so much that He made us alive with Christ, and God's wonderful kindness is what saves us from death.

To be alive to God first means that God has transformed a person's life. The New Testament talks about having passed from death to life. Salvation comes as we become dead to sin and alive to God. Salvation changes our lives. The experience of salvation links us with the creative purposes of God and causes us to rise above our circumstances to triumph over every experience of life.

Have you experienced this new life personally? Do you have that salvation? You can have it today through faith in Jesus Christ. Through your commitment to Him, is the only way you can know what it means to be alive from the dead.

"I am alive"

I am alive because of you
I have endured the darkest days because the beacon of your light guided me through.
I am alive and well by the glory of your grace.
I am blessed by I am because I am blessed to see another day!

I am alive because you have sheltered me.
Beneath your wings is my haven, I am and that is where I want to be.
I am alive because you willed it so!
You breathed life into this empty temple and You gave me a soul!

I am alive because you died upon the cross for me.
No sacrifice is greater or paralleled than the one made at Calvary!
I am alive because you shed your blood to wipe my sins away,
Redeemed am I by I Am and grateful I am that I am able to sing this song of praise!

I am alive because you willed it so my magnificent, marvelous King!
My Lord, my Savior, my Father, my God, my Light, my Everything!
I am alive and all praises are to be given You!
Now my days of darkness are gone and the light, Oh that beautiful light, that light is plentiful.

So rejoice and praise the Lord! I am alive, alive and well I say!
Alive am I and blessed I am to see this glorious day!
I am alive.

Read Ephesians 2:4, 5; John 3: 3, 5; John 5:24; 1 John 3:14, John 2:29

Salt had two purposes in the Middle East of the first century. Because of the lack of refrigeration, salt was used to preserve food, especially meat which would quickly spoil in the hot desert environment. Believers in Christ are preservatives to the world, preserving it from the evil inherent in the society of ungodly men whose unredeemed natures are corrupted by sin.

Salt was also used then as now, as a flavor enhancer. In the same way that salt enhances the flavor of the foods it season, the followers of Christ stand out as those who "enhance" the flavor of life in this world. Christian living in obedience to Christ and under the guidance of the Holy Spirit, will inevitably influence the world for good, as salt has a positive influence on the flavors of foods when season with the right amount. So as a Christian filled with God's Sprit we are to ask Him for wisdom on how He would have us to love every person He put in our lives. Where there is strife, we are to be peace makers; where there is sorrow, we are to be the ministers of Christ binding up wounds, and where there is hatred, we are to allow the love of Christ to flow through us, and be the one to return good for evil.

Read and write Matthew 5: 11-13

We are the only physical presence of Christ on earth NOW!
The Body of Christ is the visible reminder to the world that God exists and is very much in the business of reconciling everything to Him. The whole body is supplied and nourished by Christ, the head. However, He can do nothing until we recognize He is the head. One way in which the body serves as a reminder to the world is by demonstrating the type of life humanity was created to live. We all should pray for unity for the body, and help us by your Spirit not to allow our differences of denomination, doctrine and other things to divide us. But help us to come together in the spirit of unity and love of Jesus Christ. And that every church and every member of the body of Christ is built upon, stand upon, and is deeply rooted in the Rock of Jesus Christ and the Word of the living God.

Read and write Ephesians 1:22, 23; Romans 12:4-6; 1 Corinthians 12:27
Luke 9:23

_____
_____
_____
_____
_____
_____
_____
_____
_____
_____
_____
_____
_____
_____
_____
_____
_____
_____
_____
_____
_____

God Is Light, now the message that we have heard from Jesus His' Son and announce is this: God is light, and there is no darkness at all in Him.

Jesus is the Light of the World, Jesus spoke to the Pharisees and said, "I am the light of the world," He said. "Whoever follows Me will have the light of life and will never walk in darkness." However, the command I now write you is new, because its truth is seen in Christ and also in you.

The darkness is passing away and the real light is already shining. If we say that we are in the light, yet hate others, we are in the darkness to this very hour. If we love others, we live in the light, and so there is nothing in us that will cause someone else to sin.

Read and write Ephesians 5:8; 1 John 1:5-10

"Jesus has *delivered us from the power of darkness*. He has rescued us from the state of heathenish darkness and wickedness. He hath saved us from the dominion of sin, which is darkness from the dominion of Satan, who is the *prince of darkness* and from the damnation of hell, which is *utter darkness*," They are *called out of darkness*." "God hath *translated us into the kingdom of His dear Son*, brought us into the gospel-state, and made us members of the church of Christ, which is a state of light and purity." *You were once darkness, but now are you light in the Lord. Who hath called you out of darkness into His marvelous light?* Those were made willing subjects of Christ who were the slaves of Satan.

The conversion of a sinner is the translation of a soul into the kingdom of Christ out of the kingdom of the devil. The power of sin is shaken off, and the power of Christ submitted to, the law of the Spirit of life in Christ Jesus delivered us free from the law of sin and death.

Read and write Colossians 1:12-13; 1 John 1:6; 1 Peter2:9

_____

_____

_____

_____

_____

_____

_____

_____

_____

_____

_____

_____

_____

_____

_____

_____

_____

_____

_____

_____

_____

The word "forgive" means to wipe the slate clean, to pardon, to cancel a debt. As a Christian when we sin or wrong someone, we seek the forgiveness in order for our relationship to be restored with the God the Father and our Lord Jesus. We must remember that forgiveness is not granted because a person deserves to be forgiven. No one deserves to be forgiven. Forgiveness is an act of love, mercy, and grace. Forgiveness is a decision to not hold something against another person or yourself; despite what they have done to you or what you have done. Forgive other as well forgive yourself.

God sent His Son so that we may be forgiven. Walking in forgiveness let us know we belong to Jesus and love Him.

Read and write Colossians 1:14; Romans 4:7; 1 John 2:12;
Mark 11:25; Luke 17:3-4

_____

_____

_____

_____

_____

_____

_____

_____

_____

_____

_____

_____

_____

_____

_____

_____

_____

_____

_____

_____

_____

_____

_____

The Hebrew word translated broken is a strong word it means "wrecked, shattered, even crippled or maimed." Psalm 51, written by King David, characteristics associated with such brokenness include; Acknowledgment of wrong: a person with a broken spirit does not make excuses or blame others. He takes full responsibility for his wrongdoing. A broken spirit produces genuine sorrow and remorseful and a repentant heart for disobeying God's commands.

Suffering can change us, and have a broken and contrite heart. The question is: does it make us bitter or better people? By walking with God in our suffering, I believe we can be changed for the better. As Christians we should pray that God will use the tool of suffering to deliver from the sin in our lives to make us more like Jesus. This is not to say that all our suffering is caused by our own personal sin. *"Pain and suffering are not necessarily signs of God's anger: they may be exactly the opposite"* (John Blanchard). In God's hands, suffering can be used to prune us - removing the bits in our lives which aren't flourishing. The Bible put it like this:

Read and write Hebrew 12: 10-11 and Read Psalms 51

_____
_____
_____
_____
_____
_____
_____
_____
_____
_____
_____
_____
_____
_____
_____
_____
_____
_____

Humility is the path to death, because in death it gives the highest proof of its perfection. Humility is the blossom of which death to self is perfect fruit. Jesus humbled Himself unto death and opened the path in which we too must walk. As there was no way for Jesus to prove His surrender to God to the uttermost or to give up and rise out of His human nature to the glory of the Father, but through death, so it is with us too. Humility must lead us to die to self. This is the only way we can prove we have given ourselves to God. Then and only then will we find the path to life in Christ Jesus. You may ask, "How can I die self?" The death to self is not your work; it is God's work. We are to humble ourselves under the mighty hands of God and He will give us the grace we need to die to self and walk in a sprit of humility. As we acknowledge our sins and ask for His help.

Read and write 1 Peter 5:5, 6; Philippians 2:8; James 4:6 - 10

_____
_____
_____
_____
_____
_____
_____
_____
_____
_____
_____
_____
_____
_____
_____
_____
_____
_____
_____
_____
_____
_____
_____
_____

God's Everlasting Covenant of Grace. There is infinite value in the atoning blood of the Lamb of God. The new covenant with the LORD God is ratified by the blood of Jesus Christ. The "blood of the eternal covenant" with Jesus Christ stands over against "the blood of bulls and of goats" in the old covenant with Israel. Christ shed His precious blood in fulfillment of the stipulation of the everlasting covenant. Christ's atoning blood is the foundation of this covenant with God. The eternal salvation of sinful men and women is guaranteed by this eternal covenant in the blood of Jesus Christ. The everlasting guarantee of the covenant of grace is the shed blood of Jesus Christ. It is by His blood that all our sins are cancelled, justice of God was satisfied, and the law was honored. Christ has done everything that God can demand. The blood of Jesus Christ is the fulfillment of the debtor's side of the covenant. Because of the atoning sacrifice of Jesus Christ on the sinner's behalf, God is bound by His own covenant to show grace and mercy to all whom Christ redeemed by His blood. Jesus' death is the "Divine Seal of the Covenant."

This "eternal covenant" is not a covenant of works, but is a covenant of free grace that was made between God the Father, God the Son and God the Holy Spirit before the foundation of the world. In this covenant within the Trinity, Christ stood in the covenant as man's representative because man at that time did not exist. This covenant of grace was established in eternity, put into force at Calvary by the death of Jesus Christ, and sealed to the hearts of God's elect by the Holy Spirit. We receive the blessings of this covenant by faith in Christ.

God the Son, in His own blood, paid the debt of all the elect of God. He suffered the full payment of divine wrath against the sinner. No question remains; it has all been paid in full. "The wages of sin is death," and our divine substitute paid the debt in full.

Read Matthew 26:28; 2 Corinthians 3:6; Hebrews 7:22; 8:6-10; 10:16-17; 12:24; 13:20; 2 Timothy 1:9;   Write Hebrews 13:20-21

_____
_____
_____
_____
_____
_____
_____
_____
_____
_____
_____
_____
_____

Day 21   *I am a new creation!*

Because of being a new creation: I Confess and Acknowledge!

I am a new creation in Christ, old things have passed away and behold all things have been made new. I am no longer an addict of any kind, because I belong to Christ Jesus. (2 Cor. 5:17)

Jesus is Lord over my spirit, my soul and body. My body is anointed to be healed, my soul is anointed to be obedient, my spirit is anointed to be strong
(1 Thess. 5:23)

I can do all things through Christ who strengthens me (Phil. 4:13)

He who is in me is greater than he who is in the world (1 John 4:4)

No weapon formed against me can prosper (Isaiah 54:17)

I am the body of Christ. I am redeemed from the curse, because Jesus carried my sicknesses and diseases in His body on the cross and by His stripes I am healed. I forbid any sickness or disease to operate in my body. Every organ and every tissue of my body must function in the perfection in which God created it to function. I honor God and bring glory to Him in my body.
(Gal. 3:13, Mat. 8:17, 1 Peter 2:24, 1 Cor. 6:20, Isaiah 53:4-5)

I have the mind of Christ and hold the thoughts, feelings and purposes of His heart.
(1 Cor. 2:16)

The Lord is my Shepherd, I will not lack. My God supplies all my needs according to His riches in glory in Christ. (PS. 23, Phil. 4:19)

I do not have a fret or anxiety about anything nor do I have a care.
(Phil. 4:6, 1 Peter 5:6-7)

I am a believer and not a doubter. I hold fast to my confession of faith. I decide to walk by faith and practice faith. My faith comes by hearing and hearing the Word of God. Jesus is the Author and Developer of my faith. (Heb. 4:14, 11:6, 12:12, Rom. 10:17)

I fear not for God has given me a spirit of power, love and a sound mind. God is on my side. (2 Tim. 1:7, Rom. 8:31)

I let the Word dwell in me richly. He who began a good work in me will continue until the day of Christ. (Col. 3:16, Phil. 1:6)

I will submit to God and resist the devil that he must flee. (James 4:7)

I tread upon the serpents and scorpions and over all the power of the enemy. I take my shield of faith and quench his every fiery dart. (Psalm 91:13)

Samuel said, "Hath the LORD as great delight in burnt offerings and sacrifices, as in obeying the voice of the LORD? Behold, to obey is better than sacrifice, and to hearken than the fat of rams." (1 Samuel 15:22 KJV)

Sacrifice is a noble thing. As a matter of fact, Jesus Christ is our ultimate example of what it means to sacrifice. He is the perfect sacrifice, as the writer of Hebrews describes. In John's Gospel, Jesus Christ tells us that laying down one's life for another is the ultimate expression of love. Many people in scripture are noted for their acts of sacrifice for the cause of Christ and the Kingdom of God. Today's teaching is not a criticism of sacrificial acts of giving, worship, and love. But it is a caution, that sacrifice is not a substitute for obedience. When Jesus began His ministry and started to explain the nature of the Kingdom of God, He warned that there must be a righteousness that exceeds that of the Pharisees. Christ's ethical teachings contained in the Sermon on the Mount are probing and challenging. One of the reasons this is so, is because Christ deals not only with the outward expressions of obedience, but the inner workings and motivations of the heart.

Read 1 Samuel chapter 14 and 15; Matthew chapter 5
Write Matthew 5:20: In your own words what does this verse mean to you?

_____
_____
_____
_____
_____
_____
_____
_____
_____
_____
_____
_____
_____
_____
_____
_____
_____

To fulfill the high calling which God has placed upon us in creating us and redeeming us, we must have the right inner substance or character. We must come to grips with who we really are, inside and out. We *will* do what we are. So we will need to become the kind of people who habitually and straight- forwardly walk in the goodness and power of Jesus our Master and Lord. For this, a process of "spiritual formation"—really, *trans*formation—is required.

Spiritual formation for the Christian is a Spirit-driven process of forming the inner world of the human self –our "spiritual" side—in such a way that it becomes like the inner being of Christ Himself. In the degree to which such a spiritual transformation to inner Christlikeness is successful, the outer life of the individual will become a natural expression or outflow of the character and teachings of Jesus. We will simply "walk the walk," as we talk the talk. Faith without word is dead.

Write the Scripture that match: Heb. 12:1-2;   Luke 6:43-45;   Eph. 4:1

1. "Walk in a manner worthy of the calling with which you have been called."_____
2. "Since we stand before so great a cloud of witnesses, let us lay aside every encumbrance, and the sin which so easily entangles us, and let us run with endurance the race that is set before us, with our eyes set on Jesus, who initiated our faith and will bring it to perfection." _____
3. "There is no good tree which produces bad fruit....
   the good man out of the good stored up in his heart, brings forth what is good." _____

Read and write Romans 12:12

_____

_____

_____

_____

_____

_____

_____

_____

_____

Just think if an employer could say that to his employee. I was in the business world, I had hundreds of employees. Sometimes we would put an ad in the paper for a job. Well, a person would come and apply for the job. The person had to agree to work for you, but they couldn't force themselves on you. So, in the final analysis the employer could say, "You didn't choose me, I chose you." In other words, you can't make me hire you. On the other hand, the employer couldn't make the employee work for him either. You couldn't force him to do that. That would be slave labor. So, it was a question of who really has the ultimate say in this. Of course, God has the ultimate say in our salvation—No man can come to me except the Father draws him, Jesus said. But He draws everybody, He desires, He is not willing that any should perish, and He would have all men come to the knowledge of the truth.

Read and write 2 Thessalonians 2:13; John 15:16; II Timothy 1:19

_____

_____

_____

_____

_____

_____

_____

_____

_____

_____

_____

_____

_____

_____

_____

_____

_____

_____

_____

Webster's Dictionary simply defines longsuffering as "patiently enduring wrongs or difficulties," and defines patience as "the capacity to endure hardship, difficulty, or inconvenience without complaint" and "calmness, self-control, and the willingness or ability to tolerate delay." Our language section on "Longsuffering and Patience" briefly defines the meaning of some of the key biblical words related to this fruit, but these definitions require further expansion if we are to truly understand what it means to be patient and longsuffering.

In the Bible, the Greek word *makrothymia* refers to being patient and loving in our relations with people. For example, St. Paul tells St. Timothy that he should exhort his congregations "with longsuffering and doctrine." St. Paul further encourages the Christians at Ephesus to exhibit "longsuffering, bearing with one another in love, endeavoring to keep the unity of the Spirit in the bond of peace."

The Greek word *hypomone* refers to dealing patiently with things or circumstances. This is the word used by St. Paul in his exhortation to be "patient in tribulation," and to "run with patience [or endurance] the race that is set before us"

God is longsuffering toward us specifically so that we can repent and turn to Him.

Hear in the case of the Apostle Paul, His mercy and truth, Paul who was first Saul the persecutor. He needed mercy, and he has said that it was shown towards him: 'I who was before a blasphemer, and a persecutor, and injurious: but I obtained mercy, that in me Christ Jesus might show forth all longsuffering towards those who shall believe in Him unto life eternal.' So that, when Paul received pardon of such great crimes, no one should despair of any sins whatever being forgiven him. Lo! Thou hast Mercy.

Read 2 Timothy 4:2; Ephesians 4:2-3; 1Timothy 1:12-16:
Write Hebrews 12:1; Romans 12:12;

_____

_____

_____

_____

_____

_____

_____

_____

_____

_____

When a person is crucified, he dies, if that is the case how then do now live? We live now because Christ was raised from the dead, and we too are raised from the dead, to newness of life in Him. Christ now lives in us.

God is a real person and our relationship with Him can be cultivated as with any other relationship. We have been saved to live in fellowship with Him. We can enjoy the riches of the Christian life only as we grow in intimacy with Christ. The presence of our Lord in our lives brings this intimacy and these riches in glory with Him. When we are crucified with Christ we allow Him to strip away everything that keeps us from having an intimate fellowship with Him. It is like letting Him strip off all our old worn out clothing and letting Him robe us in His perfect righteousness. Anything that would keep us from following into the fullness of His life needs to be nailed to the cross daily. Take your place on the cross.

Read and write Galatians 2: 20; Galatians 5:24-25

Day 27 *I am justified!*

Justification is an act of God the Father. God renders a verdict regarding the one who believes in Christ. "It is God who justifies." Justification removes the guilt of sin and clothes the believer with Christ's perfect righteousness, thus entitling him to eternal life in God's own family. Justification is an act of God obtained by or through faith. "There is one God who will justify the circumcised by faith and the uncircumcised through faith." Faith is not the ground or cause of justification but the instrument by which the believer receives justification. Faith is the gift of God which lays hold of and receives what Christ has accomplished. The believer's salvation and justification are totally a work of God.

Read and write Titus 3:5 -7; Read Romans chapter 8

I am a soldier in the army of my God. The Lord Jesus Christ is my commanding officer. The Holy Bible is my code of conduct. Faith, prayer, and the Word are my weapons of warfare. I have been taught by the Holy Spirit, trained by experience, tried by adversity and tested by fire. I am a volunteer in this army, and I am enlisted for eternity. Take your share of the hardships *and* suffering [which you are called to endure] as a good (first-class) soldier of Christ Jesus. We are spiritual soldiers and the fight is against the devil and not people. We are told to put on God's whole armor [the armor of a heavy-armed soldier which God supplies], that you may be able successfully to stand up against [all] the strategies *and* the deceits of the devil. So put on God's armor now! Then when the evil day comes, you will be able to resist the enemy's attacks; and after fighting to the end, you will still hold your ground. Stand ready, with truth as a belt tight around your waist, with righteousness as your breastplate, and as your shoes the readiness to announce the Good News of peace. At all times carry faith as a shield; for with it you will be able to put out all the burning arrows shot by the Evil One. And accept salvation as a helmet, and the word of God as the sword which the Spirit gives you. Do all this in prayer, asking for God's help. Pray on every occasion, as the Spirit leads. For this reason keep alert and never give up; pray always for all God's people.

Read and write Titus 3:5-7; Read Ephesians 6:10-21

_____
_____
_____
_____
_____
_____
_____
_____
_____
_____
_____
_____
_____
_____
_____
_____

What Is Sanctification? Sanctification (Greek: hagiasmos) means literally "making holy". It also means "consecration" or "setting apart" something for a special holy purpose.   As a Christian, sanctification has two parts - God's part and ours. In many things in the Christian life God is playing the major role - and yet we have our part to do also - which is to respond in faith and obedience to what God is saying. In sanctification, our part is to offer to God our bodies as a living sacrifice - in fact to consciously offer our whole spirit, soul and body completely to God so that we devote ourselves to forever do His will and not our own. Our sanctification cannot be complete than the sincerity and the understanding with which we make this dedication to God. God's part in our sanctification is to actually change us by the operation of His blood, His Word and His Spirit. We are sanctified by God's grace - his unmerited favor working in our hearts and lives. We have to trust God to work in us. He is the One who produces godly character in us, the fruit of the Spirit and the ability to overcome sin consistently.

Sanctification can also be defined as: "possessing the mind of Christ, and all the mind of Christ." God wants us to allow our minds to be renewed our thinking and attitudes must change if we are to grow in God. Many of our thinking patterns, values and priorities have been shaped by the world system and not by God. We must relearn many things. "We have the mind of Christ" legally. But to actually think Christ's thoughts and allow Him to rule our behavior we will need to submit to the work of the Holy Spirit so as to appropriate our inheritance in this area.

Sanctification also relates to emotional healing, or a changed heart and holiness also means the development of the fruit of the Holy Spirit,

Read and write Hebrews 2:11; Romans 12:1,2; Ephesians 4:23; 1 Corinthians 2:16;

_____

_____

_____

_____

_____

_____

_____

_____

_____

_____

_____

_____

_____

_____

_____

_____

A reconciled person acts upon new principles, by new rules, with new ends, and in new company. The believer is created anew; his heart is not merely set right, but a new heart is given him. He is the workmanship of God, created in Christ Jesus unto good works. He is changed in his character and conduct. These words must and do mean more than an outward reformation. The man who formerly saw no beauty in the Savior that he should desire Him. Now loves Him above all things.

The heart of the unregenerate, not reborn spiritually and not repentant is filled with enmity against God, and God is justly, and rightly offended with him. Yet there may be reconciliation. Our offended God has reconciled us to Himself by Jesus Christ. By the inspiration of God, the Scriptures were written, which are the word of reconciliation; showing that peace has been made by the cross, and how we may be interested in God's peace and this new life He has for us. God cannot lose by the quarrel, nor gain by the peace, yet He beseeches sinners to lay aside their enmity, hostility and antagonism and accept the salvation He offers.

Christ knew no sin. He was made Sin; not a sinner, but Sin, a Sin-offering, a Sacrifice for sin. The end and design of all this was, that we might be made the righteousness of God in Him, might be justified freely by the grace of God through the redemption which is in Christ Jesus. Can any lose, anything, or suffer too much for Him, who gave His beloved Son to be the Sacrifice for our sins, that we might be made the righteousness of God in Him?

Read and write 2 Corinthians 5:18-19

_____
_____
_____
_____
_____
_____
_____
_____
_____
_____
_____
_____
_____
_____
_____

Our heavenly Father said, "We can come to HIS throne of grace to obtain help in a time of need for healing and restoration in our body". And He desire above all things that we would prosper and be in good health. Healing is one of the benefits that you have because of being God's child and He is your Father.

Jehovah Rapha has healed you because of the stripes of Jesus Christ, no plague, sickness or disease shall come nigh your dwelling. God has taken sickness and disease away from you and the number of your days He will fulfill. And because of the Lord Jesus you can confess and decree, "I am whole, well and sound in my spirit, soul, body and mind.

Read and write Psalms 103: 2-5; Psalms 103: 2-5; Hebrews 4:16; Isaiah 53:5; Matthew 16:19

I am thankful to Christ Jesus our Lord. He has given me strength. I thank him that he considered me faithful. And I thank him for appointing me to serve him. I used to speak evil things against Jesus. I tried to hurt his followers. I really pushed them around. But God showed me mercy anyway. I did those things without knowing any better. I wasn't a believer. Our Lord poured out more and more of his grace on me. Along with it came faith and love from Christ Jesus. Here is a saying that you can trust. It should be accepted completely. Christ Jesus came into the world to save sinners. And I am the worst sinner of all. But for that very reason, God showed me mercy. And I am the worst of sinners. He showed me mercy so that Christ Jesus could show that he is very patient. I was an example for those who would come to believe in him. Then they would receive eternal life. The eternal King will never die. He can't be seen. He is the only God. Give him honor and glory for ever and ever. Amen   1 Timothy 1:12-17 (NIRV)

What are you thankful for?

_____

_____

_____

_____

_____

_____

_____

_____

_____

_____

_____

_____

_____

_____

_____

_____

_____

_____

_____

A Christian disciple is a person who develops a personal, lifelong, obedient relationship with Jesus Christ. In which Christ transforms your character into Christlikeness; changes your values into kingdom values; and involves you in the home, the church and the world. By practicing these biblical principles you can be useful in the Master's service.

Avery T. Wills, Jr. The Disciple's Cross (Master Life)

Then He said to them all: "If anyone would come after me, he must deny himself and take up his cross daily and follow me.

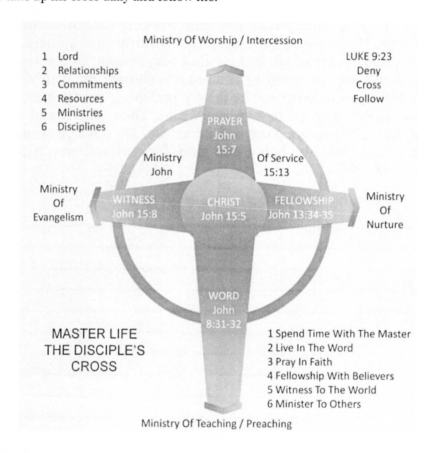

Ministry Of Worship / Intercession

1	Lord
2	Relationships
3	Commitments
4	Resources
5	Ministries
6	Disciplines

LUKE 9:23
Deny
Cross
Follow

PRAYER John 15:7

Ministry John   Of Service 15:13

Ministry Of Evangelism

WITNESS John 15:8   CHRIST John 15:5   FELLOWSHIP John 13:34-35

Ministry Of Nurture

WORD John 8:31-32

MASTER LIFE THE DISCIPLE'S CROSS

1 Spend Time With The Master
2 Live In The Word
3 Pray In Faith
4 Fellowship With Believers
5 Witness To The World
6 Minister To Others

Ministry Of Teaching / Preaching

We have one Lord. We worship Him, Glorify Him, and put Him in the centre of our lives. This means that all else – our family, our career, our dearest hobby, etc. are secondary. *Read and write John 15:5*

_____

_____

_____

_____

We have two relationships. A vertical relationship with God; And horizontal relationship with fellow men, through fellowship with believers and reaching out to pre-believers.

We have three commitments. Deny, Cross, Follow: *Read and write Luke 9:23*

_____

_____

_____

_____

We have four resources to help us as we learn to walk with Christ on the basis of the three commitments.

We pray to the Lord for grace, to help and guide us: *Read and write John 15:7* _____

_____

_____

We read and meditate on His Word (Bible) daily to be renewed and to receive understanding of His Will for us. *Read and write John 8:31-32*

_____

_____

_____

_____

_____

_____

_____

We have fellowship with believers, and in the process encourage and exalt one another to follow after Christ. *Read and Write John 13:34-35*

_____

_____

_____

_____

_____

_____

_____

_____

_____

We witness to pre-believers through telling them about God's love and through our lifestyle (lifestyle evangelism). *Read and write John 15:8*

_____

_____

_____

_____

We have five ministries to serve as we grow with the Lord. *The ministry of worship / intercession,* in which we intercede in prayer for others who are in need/ *The ministry of nurture,* in which we help fellow young believers to grow in the knowledge and grace of God. *The ministry of teaching / preaching:* in which we deliver the message of God and his salvation to all. *The ministry of evangelism,* in which we reach out to pre-believers and tell them about the gospel and the sacrificial love of Christ in order that we all may be saved. *The ministry of service:* as we serve one another and continue to grow one another in the love of Christ.

We have six disciplines. To grow as Christ's disciples, we must be disciplined. *First,* we must continue to have Christ at the centre of our lives. *Second,* we must consistently pray to Him, for grace, for guidance, for help and for His will in our lives and directions. *Third,* we must read His Word (Bible) in order to understand and know what He wants of us – in terms of obedience and guidance. *Fourth,* we must continually fellowship with believers and to constantly uphold and uplift one another. *Fifth,* we reach out to non-believers with the love of Christ so that they know of Christ in us. *Sixth,* as we grow as Christ disciples, we begin to serve in ministries that He wants us to be in.

If I speak in the tongues of men or of angels, but do not have love, I am only a resounding gong or a clanging cymbal. If I have the gift of prophecy and can fathom all mysteries and all knowledge, and if I have a faith that can move mountains, but do not have love, I am nothing. If I give all I possess to the poor and give over my body to hardship that I may boast, but do not have love, I gain nothing. Love is patient, love is kind. It does not envy, it does not boast, it is not proud. It does not dishonor others, it is not self-seeking, it is not easily angered, it keeps no record of wrongs. Love does not delight in evil but rejoices with the truth. It always protects, always trusts, always hopes, always perseveres.

Love never fails. But where there are prophecies, they will cease; where there are tongues, they will be stilled; where there is knowledge, it will pass away. For we know in part and we prophesy in part, but when completeness comes, what is in part disappears. [1] When I was a child, I talked like a child I thought like a child, I reasoned like a child. When I became a man, I put the ways of childhood behind me. [1] For now we see only a reflection as in a mirror; then we shall see face to face. Now I know in part; then I shall know fully, even as I am fully known. And now these three remain: faith, hope and love. But the greatest of these is love. (1Cor. 13:1-13)

Read and write 1 John 2: 8-11

_____
_____
_____
_____
_____
_____
_____
_____
_____
_____
_____
_____
_____
_____
_____
_____

According to God's Word "beloved, I pray that in all respects you may prosper and be in good health, just as your soul prospers."(3 John 2)

True Prosperity

In order to prosper, you must first have a prosperous soul. That's the beginning of the prosperous life. But how do you get there? That kind of prosperous life doesn't just happen. And it doesn't happen overnight.

Foundation for true prosperity:

◊ **Seek first:** What did Jesus tell us to seek first?
Read and write Matthew 6:33

_____

_____

_____

_____

_____

_____

◊ **Walk in truth**: That means walking in the light of God's Word, according to His ways, His wisdom, what He says is right.   *Read and write John 8:31-32*

_____

_____

_____

_____

_____

_____

_____

◊ **Faithfulness and Diligence:** The force of faithfulness is a fruit of the spirit that you received when you were born again. Webster's dictionary defines *faithful* as "full of faith, believing, strong or firm in one's faith, firmly adhering to duty, a true fidelity, loyal, true to allegiance, constant in the performance of duties or services."
Read and write Matthew 25:21

_____

_____

_____

◇ **Tithing and Sowing:** Tithing is a covenant transaction that gets God involved in what you are doing. The first 10 percent of your income—the tithe—belongs to God. The Bible calls it first fruits. It's devoted to God, and it goes to support ministries that feed you spiritually.
Read Malachi 3:8-10

_____
_____
_____
_____
_____
_____
_____
_____
_____
_____
_____
_____
_____
_____
_____
_____

◇ **Believing and Saying**: Faith must be in two places—in your heart and in your mouth. "The word is nigh thee, even in thy mouth, and in thy heart: that is, the word of faith, which we preach" (Believing in your heart and saying with your mouth produce the operation of faith.
Read II Corinthians 4:13; Romans 10:8- 13

_____
_____
_____
_____
_____
_____
_____
_____

Day 38, 39 & 40
Faith comes by hearing and confessing and living God's Word.

Lord, cause my understanding to become enlightened in the things that I do not understand and in things I cannot foresee.

I trust in the Lord with all my understanding for His directions and instructions and I do not lean or rely on my own righteousness or my own understanding.

I am the son of God and am lead by His Spirit.

I have the Spirit of truth within me. He guides and leads me in all things and points me in the right direction. And whenever I do not know what to say the Holy Spirit teaches me and tell me what to say.

I have put on the new man. I have been born of God and created in His image and in His righteousness to live a life that is holy and pleasing unto Him.

I put on the full armor of God, so that when the day of evil comes, I am able to stand my ground, and after I have done everything, to stand.

I stand firm then, with the belt of truth buckled around my waist, with the breastplate of righteousness in place, and with your feet fitted with the readiness that comes from the gospel of peace. In addition to all this, I take up the shield of faith, with which I will extinguish all the flaming arrows of the evil one. I take the helmet of salvation and the sword of the Spirit, which is the word of God.

I pray in the Spirit on all occasions with all kinds of prayers and requests. With this in mind, I am alert and always keep praying for all my brothers and sisters in Jesus.

I pray and thank you Father God, also that whenever I speak, words may be given me by Your Holy Spirit so that I will fearlessly make known the mystery of the gospel, for which I am an ambassador in this world and Pray that I may declare it fearlessly, as I should.

This life I now live I am able to live in victoriously by the power, faith and strength of the Son of God, who loves me, and gave His life for me.

I stand strong and unmovable in victory and with this liberty which can because of Christ Jesus.

I stand firm and strong in the liberty by which Christ Jesus has made me free from the power of sin and death.

I am submitted unto God and to His Word and the Spirit of God. Therefore I have the power through Christ Jesus to resist the devil and then he flees from me.

Jesus Christ has given me the keys to the kingdom which is the power and authority of His Word. Jesus gave me the authority to use His name. I have the authority to the word of God to speak to my mountains.

Jesus is the anointed one by God and He has placed His anointing upon my life. I am the righteousness of God created in Christ Jesus.

As I speak the Word of God they are no longer my words, but GOD'WORD. And therefore, the Word of God that I speak cannot and shall no return void, but shall accomplish and strike the mark of that in which it is sent (through my prayer and confessions) to perform.

I am a doer of the Word and not just a hearer. I believe in the Word of God. I trust in the Word and I confidently stand upon the Word of God. I am what the Word says I am, and I can do what the Word says I can do. I have by faith the blessings of the Lord upon my life that the Word declares are mine. I have God's Spirit upon me. His power and His presence exude through me.

God has given me a commission I confess that everywhere I go that signs follow me. The Word of God has declared to me that these signs follow them that believe. And because I am a believer I receive miracles, signs, and wonders following me, exemplifying that I am a believer who has been washed by the blood of Jesus Christ, and filled with His Holy Spirit. I am the temple of the Holy Spirit. By the power and authority of Jesus Christ, these signs follow me: I cast out demons and devils; I speak with new tongues; I lay hands upon the sick and they do recover from sickness and diseases.

I abide and remain in Christ and Christ abides and remains in me. I am created in His likeness; I diligently confess God's Word over my life so my mind, lifestyle, and action become conformed and changed, and transformed into Christ likeness. In His authority and power so as an ambassador to represent Him in the earth. I seek first God's kingdom and His righteousness, and all these things will be given to me. To rule, reign, and dominate in the earth.

God has anointed me as a king. I am a king unto the most High King, "Jesus Christ", and therefore my words have power and authority as, "The Most High King Jesus." Jesus is seated in heavenly places with all things under

His feet. I am in Christ all things are under my feet. So whatever I decree and declare in the spiritual realm is established and manifested in the physical realm. So I make these declarations: sickness, disease, poverty, lack, and insufficiency, every demonic principality, power, ruler of darkness of this world and spiritual wickedness in high places are all under my feet, and have no power over my life and the lives of my family.

As a king, I decree that every promise in the Word of God is mine. I study God's Word to know what belong to me. I grow daily in the grace of God and in the knowledge, understanding and faith of Jesus Christ.

As a king I and reign over devil, demon, demonic spirit force and principality. As a king unto Christ Jesus, I decree and declare them to be off limits to my life and the lives of my family.

As a king, I decree that only the will of God is done in my life. I decree that Satan's will of killing, stealing, and destruction is prohibited and bound from my life. Only the will of God, which is to give me life and life more abundantly is performed and manifested in my life.

As a king I am a vessel of honor unto the Lord. I have been purged by the Holy Spirit and have been sanctified, prepared and available for the Lord good work.

As a king my weapons of prayer and confession of the Word of God are not carnal but mighty through God. By the authority of the Word of God in Christ Jesus, I pull down strongholds and cast down every imaginations and every high thing that exalts itself against the knowledge of God. I bring into captivity every unrighteous, immoral and ungodly thought to the obedience of Christ Jesus my Lord and Most High King.

Notes_____

_____

_____

_____

_____

_____

_____

_____

_____

_____

_____